© Copyright 2015 by Charles Treft

Dedicated to Lily and Adalay, my two beautiful granddaughters

It was a bright sunny morning as Celeste was awakened by her dog Lady licking her cheeks letting her know it was time to get up for school. Celeste raced to the bathroom to brush her teeth and to comb her hair. As she brushed her teeth she thought about how much she loved her school, The Alpaca Lane Criations Elementary School. She could hardly wait to see her teacher, Mr. Chockablock, and her best friends Tootsie, Champ, Blue and Bella.

Celeste's first class at school each morning was Reading. The school principal, Mr. Chico, usually walked through the classrooms during this time to see if the boys and girls were getting really smart. Today, he asked Celeste to read a book to him. She chose the book, *You want us to do what Mr. Chockablock?* It was one of her favorites because the author had written a story about how her classmates and herself were getting really smart in school by Giving their best, Owning their learning, Always being ready to learn, Loving to Learn and Striving for Excellence.

The morning flew by and at 11:30 Mr. Chockablock told the boys and girls it was time for recess. Mr. Chockablock asked the boys and girls to line up, and as usual, Champ tried to be the line leader and Bella always wanted to be the caboose. "5 – 4 – 3 – 2 – 1 are we ready to go boys and girls?" asked Mr. Chockablock. "I can't find my hat Mr. Chockablock," said Blue. "Did you look in your backpack and around your desk Blue?" asked Mr. Chockablock. "Yes, but it's not here," said Blue. The students helped Blue look for his hat. After a couple of minutes, Turbo blurted out, "Oh here it is, I found it under Blue's desk!" Turbo handed Blue his hat, but not before stepping on it with his foot and telling him he was a loser. This wasn't the first time Turbo had done something mean to Blue or to one of his other classmates.

At recess, Celeste, Champ, Bella, Blue and Tootsie played on the monkey bars. Champ hung upside down from the monkey bars even though he had been told a hundred times by Mr. Chockablock it was unsafe. Mrs. Splashes, the other recess teacher, saw Champ hanging upside down from the monkey bars and blew her whistle to get his attention. Champ lost 5 minutes of his recess for not following the playground rules.

At noon, Mrs. Splashes blew her whistle to let the students know recess was over. The boys and girls quickly lined up to go inside for lunch. "Mrs. Splashes, my red hat is gone, I took it off when I was playing on the monkey bars and now it is gone!" said Blue. Mrs. Splashes looked around the playground and spotted a red hat up in the tree next to the basketball hoop. She once again blew her whistle to get the students' attention. "Who threw Blue's red hat up in the tree?" asked Mrs. Splashes. Everyone had a good idea of who had thrown Blue's hat up into the tree, but the students were afraid to tell Mrs. Splashes. It wasn't the first time a student's hat, gloves or scarf had ended up in the tree.

"We will wait here all day if we have to, but someone is going to tell me who threw Blue's hat up in the tree," said Mrs. Splashes. Finally Celeste told Mrs. Splashes that she had seen Turbo throw Blue's hat up into the tree. Turbo glared at Celeste and called her a "Snitch."

Turbo made mean faces at Celeste the rest of the afternoon in the classroom. There were several times he bumped into her as she sat at her desk. One time when Turbo walked by Celeste's desk, he told her she was ugly and that her mother was even uglier. Celeste didn't say anything to Turbo and for the first time in her life she didn't want to be in school. Celeste asked Mr. Chockablock if she could go to the bathroom. She could feel the tears starting to fall on her cheeks. She couldn't wait to go to the bathroom so the other students wouldn't see her crying.

When Celeste got on the bus that afternoon, the bus driver could tell she wasn't her normal happy self. The bus driver thought maybe she was just tired. As soon as Celeste got home, she ran into her bedroom and wanted nothing more than to just be by herself. She kept hearing Turbo telling her she was ugly and that her mom was uglier and that she was a snitch. If that wasn't bad enough, she was afraid Turbo might try to hurt her and she didn't know what to do to make him stop. Celeste decided to not tell her mother about the mean things Turbo had done to her and hoped tomorrow would be a better day. Her dreams that night were not the normal dreams that ended with "Happily ever after." She kept seeing and hearing Turbo saying mean things to her.

The next day at school, Celeste decided she would stay as far away from Turbo as she could. It wasn't long before Turbo came up to her and told her she had the biggest teeth he had ever seen. If that wasn't bad enough, he asked her why she wore clothes from the dumpster. Celeste could feel the tears starting to well up in her eyes, but she decided if she acted tough and continued to ignore Turbo he would stop. Blue overheard Turbo tell Celeste that she had big teeth and that her clothes were from the dumpster. He wanted to say or do something, but he was afraid of Turbo. Turbo was the biggest student in his class.

Celeste, Tootsie, Champ, Blue and Bella raced to the monkey bars for recess. They were surprised to see Turbo waiting for them. Celeste and Blue hid behind Champ, Tootsie and Bella hoping Turbo wouldn't see them. "I see you guys are playing with a couple of losers," said Turbo. Champ, Tootsie and Bella were afraid of Turbo, so they didn't say anything back to him. They had seen how Turbo had treated Celeste and Blue the day before. They felt helpless and just wished Turbo would go play somewhere else on the playground.

Turbo walked up to Celeste and pushed her to the ground. Celeste started to cry. Turbo called her a cry baby and told her he had never seen someone with such big, floppy, crooked ears. It seemed like hours to Tootsie, Champ, Blue, Bella and Celeste as they waited for Mrs. Splashes to blow her whistle to end recess.

Things didn't get any better for Celeste during lunch. Turbo walked up to her and poked his finger into her cheeseburger. Blue, Champ, Tootsie and Bella watched helplessly not knowing what they should do. Celeste didn't want Turbo to be mean to her or anyone else, so she decided to ask Mrs. Coco, the school counselor, for help. She asked Blue if he wanted to go with her, but Blue told her he was afraid Turbo might see him going to Mrs. Coco's office and really get mad at him.

After lunch, Celeste asked Mr. Chockablock if she could go speak with Mrs. Coco. Celeste had talked with Mrs. Coco before and really liked how she was kind and always seemed to know what to say to make her feel better. When she arrived at Mrs. Coco's office, she began, "Mrs. Coco, Blue and I are having a problem with Turbo being mean to us. The other day, Turbo stepped on Blue's hat in class, threw his hat up in the tree at recess and called him a loser. Mrs. Splashes asked who had thrown Blue's hat into the tree and I told her it was Turbo. Since then, Turbo has been saying mean things to me, pushing me and doing other things that make me think he is going to hurt me. I am afraid of Turbo and I don't know what to do to make him stop, I used to like school, but now I just want to go home!" said Celeste. After talking with Celeste a little while longer, Mrs. Coco told Celeste that Turbo was acting like a bully. Mrs. Coco told Celeste she wanted her to tell an adult if Turbo did anything else to her at school. She also told Celeste she was going to visit Mr. Chockablock's classroom and talk to the students about what they could do if someone was acting like a bully to them.

The next day at recess there were three hats in the same tree that Blue's hat had been hanging from a couple days before. The other students had seen how Turbo was treating Celeste and Blue, so no one dared tell Mrs. Splashes that Turbo had thrown the hats up into the tree. That afternoon, Mrs. Coco, the school counselor, visited Mr. Chockablock's classroom and spoke to his students. Mrs. Coco told the students she wanted to talk to them about what they should do if someone was mean or acted like a bully to them. "First, I should tell you the difference between someone being mean to you and someone acting like a bully toward you," said Mrs. Coco. She told the class there was a difference. "Someone might call you a name or push you and then they stop, it still makes you feel bad, it is mean, but it is not bullying," explained Mrs. Coco.

"A student who acts like a bully could be someone who is bigger or stronger than you, pushes or punches you, says mean things to you hoping you will feel bad about yourself, they do these things over and over again and you don't know what to do to make them stop," said Mrs. Coco. Celeste was feeling like she could throw up at any minute, she could feel Turbo glaring at her. Blue was just hoping Turbo wouldn't look in his direction. Champ, Tootsie and Bella couldn't stop thinking about how Turbo had been treating Celeste and Blue over the last couple of days.

Mrs. Coco told the students to always tell an adult if someone was mean or acting like a bully to them. She told them they could also tell the person to STOP, that they didn't like the way they were making them feel and that they would tell an adult if they didn't stop. Mrs. Coco told the students they could also choose a secret word to say to their friends if they needed help from someone being mean or acting like a bully to them. She also told them if they saw someone being mean or acting like a bully to someone else, they should not only tell an adult, but try to help the student or friend get away from the person.

The next day at recess, Turbo grabbed Blue's hat, but this time Blue hung onto his hat. Blue remembered the strategies Mrs. Coco had taught him the day before. He told Turbo to STOP trying to take his hat. Turbo responded, "Hey Punk, You better give me your hat or I am going to punch you!" Blue told Turbo again to STOP and that if he didn't stop he would have to tell Mr. Chockablock." Celeste saw Turbo trying to take Blue's hat and immediately ran over to help, right behind her were Tootsie, Champ and Bella.

Champ, Tootsie, Celeste and Bella stood in front of Turbo. Turbo told them they had better get out of his way or he was going to hit all of them. Champ told Turbo to STOP and that he was not going to let him take Blue's hat. Tootsie said, "We won't allow you to treat or talk to us that way anymore and if you don't STOP we are going to tell Mr. Chockablock and Mrs. Splashes!" Bella said, "Blue is our friend and we won't allow you to act like a bully to him!" Celeste had a warm feeling inside knowing she had joined her friends in standing up to Turbo. Turbo could tell the students were serious and walked away, but not without first saying he didn't want to play with a bunch of losers. Champ, Celeste, Tootsie, Bella and Blue couldn't believe Mrs. Coco's strategies had worked.

That afternoon, Celeste went back to Mrs. Coco's office to let her know the good news. "Mrs. Coco, Blue, Tootsie, Champ, Bella and I stood up to Turbo today at recess and told him we were not going to allow him to act like a bully to us anymore. We were all really scared, but we did what you told us to and it worked," said Celeste. "I am really proud of you Celeste, I am glad you decided to do something today and not to be a bystander," said Mrs. Coco. "What is a bystander?" asked Celeste. Mrs. Coco told Celeste a bystander is someone who sees a person being mean or acting like a bully to someone, but doesn't do anything to stop them. Celeste felt great knowing that she had helped Blue and also herself. As she walked back to her classroom, she loved school once again.

Turbo was very quiet the rest of the day in school. The students thought he was sick. That evening at his house Turbo thought about what Mrs. Coco had told his class and how Champ, Tootsie, Bella, Blue and Celeste had stood up to him. Turbo realized he didn't want to do mean things or act like a bully to other students in school. He really just wanted to have friends who liked him, he wanted friends like Champ, Tootsie, Bella, Celeste and Blue, but he didn't know how to make friends. His family had moved a lot and just when he thought he was going to make a friend, they moved again. Turbo started to cry as he drifted off to sleep.

The next day at recess Celeste, Tootsie, Champ, Blue and Bella raced to the monkey bars. Champ hung upside down as usual, Mrs. Splashes blew her whistle to stop him and he had to stand with her for 5 minutes. One thing was different today, Turbo was actually playing tag with Blue and the recess tree didn't have any hats hanging from its branches.

The next morning as the students arrived at school, they saw their principal, Mr. Chico, standing in front of the school next to something covered up with a white sheet. The boys and girls asked Mr. Chico what was under the sheet. He told the students they would have to wait until the school assembly at 9 a.m. that morning to see what was hidden under the sheet.

At 9 a.m., Mr. Chico called the teachers over the intercom and asked them to bring their students to the front of the school. When the students arrived, Mr. Chico was standing next to the mysterious thing covered with a sheet and beside him was a box. He opened the box and pulled out several hats. "Boys and Girls a few days ago the tree on our playground had these hats hanging from it, but for the last couple of days, there haven't been any hats hanging from the tree. Yesterday at recess I took a picture of some students who just a few days ago didn't like each other, but now they are friends. Mr. Chico pulled the sheet off of the mysterious thing and the students saw a picture of Champ, Tootsie, Bella, Celeste, Blue and Turbo smiling and hugging.

Mr. Chico told the students he didn't want to see or hear any of them being mean or acting like a bully to another student at the Alpaca Lane Criations Elementary School. Mr. Chico told the students he wanted them to be kind and to treat others as they would want to be treated. He told the students he had a special surprise for them and asked the teachers to take their students around to the tree on the playground. Mr. Chico told the boys and girls to close their eyes. Tootsie, Champ, Blue and Bella had no idea that Celeste was going to help Mr. Chico with the special surprise. "I am going to count to 3 and on 3, I want you to open your eyes, 1, 2,…….3," said Mr. Chico.

The students opened their eyes to the most beautiful sight they had ever seen. The tree on the playground that used to have hats hanging from it, now had hundreds of bright, shiny, colored lights covering the branches. Mr. Chico told the boys and girls he wanted them to show kindness and treat each other the way they would want to be treated. He told them their kindness and actions would be seen by everyone just like the lights on the tree and would brighten everyone's day. The students left that day knowing they would never again allow someone to be mean or to act like a bully in their school. And lastly, Champ, Celeste, Bella, Tootsie and Blue decided their secret word to say if they needed help from someone being mean or acting like a bully to them would be "Monkey Bars".

Fun Facts About Alpacas

- Alpacas like to lay in front of fans in the summertime to stay cool
- Alpacas like to have their bellies sprayed with a water hose in the summertime
- Alpacas make a humming noise to talk to other alpacas
- Alpacas get their fiber shorn (a haircut) once a year
- An alpaca's fiber on top of their head is called a topknot
- Alpacas weigh about 14 pounds when they are born
- Alpacas eat grass and hay
- Alpacas only have bottom teeth
- Alpacas have toes
- Baby alpacas are called crias

About the Author

Charles Treft has been an educator in public education for over eighteen years. He is currently an elementary school principal with the Calvert County Public Schools in Maryland. Charles has been a classroom teacher and vice principal at the high school and elementary school levels. Charles proudly served his country in the United States Marines Corps and his community as a deputy sheriff. This is Charles's second book. The book contains messages Charles talks about each day with his students. Charles and his wife Susan raise alpacas, and in fact, the alpacas in the story live at their farm in Upper Marlboro, Maryland. Charles wants to see every student shine their light in a positive way to make someone's day a little brighter. Charles would love to visit your school and read his book to your students. Charles can be contacted at **CMT1962@aol.com**.

About the illustrator

Charlie J. Love

C.J. Love is a 2008 MICA (Maryland Institute College of Art) graduate and has a BFA in Graphic Design. C.J. Specializes in illustration, caricatures, mural painting, logo design, and web design. His website features his portfolio and other work. If you want to request work from him please visit ***www.clove2design.com*** or call him at **301-675-1643**.

Alpaca Lane Criations Elementary School

STAFF — 2015 YEARBOOK

Mr. Chico
Principal

Mrs. Coco
School Counselor

Mr. Chockablock
Teacher

Mrs. Splashes
Teacher

Alpaca Lane Criations Elementary School

Bella

Celeste

Blue

Tootsie

Champ

Turbo

Made in the USA
Middletown, DE
22 September 2015